▶▶ **FastForward**™

Riffs, ~~Licks & Tricks~~ ~~today!~~

12-BarBlues Piano

with Jack Long

PS 14

Wise Publications
London / New York / Sydney / Paris / Copenhagen / Madrid

Exclusive Distributors:
Music Sales Limited
14-15 Berners Street, London W1T 3LJ, UK.
Music Sales Pty Limited
20 Resolution Drive, Caringbah, NSW 2229, Australia.
Music Sales Corporation
257 Park Avenue South, New York, NY 10010, USA.

Order No. AM92445
ISBN 0-7119-4521-7
This book © Copyright 1997 by Wise Publications.

Book design by Michael Bell Design.
Edited and arranged by Jack Long.
Music processed by Interactive Music Sciences Limited.
Cover photography by George Taylor.
Cover instrument kindly loaned by Rose Morris Limited.
Text photographs courtesy of
London Features International and Redferns.
Printed and bound in the United Kingdom.

Your Guarantee of Quality:
As publishers, we strive to produce every book to
the highest commercial standards.
The music has been freshly engraved and the book has
been carefully designed to minimise awkward page turns
and to make playing from it a real pleasure.
Particular care has been given to specifying acid-free,
neutral-sized paper made from pulps which have not
been elemental chlorine bleached.
This pulp is from farmed sustainable forests and
was produced with special regard for the environment.
Throughout, the printing and binding have
been planned to ensure a sturdy, attractive publication
which should give years of enjoyment.
If your copy fails to meet our high standards, please
inform us and we will gladly replace it.

www.musicsales.com

Introduction

Hello, and welcome to ▶▶Fast**Forward.**

Congratulations on purchasing a product that will improve your playing and provide you with hours of pleasure. All the music in this book has been specially created by professional musicians to give you maximum value and enjoyability.

If you already know how to 'drive' your instrument but you'd like to do a little customising, you've pulled in at the right place. We'll put you on the fast track to playing the kinds of riffs and patterns that today's professionals rely on.

We'll provide you with a vocabulary of riffs that you can apply in a wide variety of musical situations, with a special emphasis on giving you the techniques that will help you in a band situation. That's why every music example in this book comes with a full-band audio track so that you get your chance to join in.

All players and all bands get their sounds and styles by drawing on the same basic building blocks.

With ▶▶Fast**Forward** you'll quickly learn these, and then be ready to use them to create your own style.

12-Bar Blues Piano

The 12-bar blues straddles such a wide variety of musical styles that it might be interesting to look briefly at how some of those different styles came about.

In 1880s and 1890s America two different kinds of black popular music developed in two different places at more or less the same time. In St. Louis they called it 'ragtime', and in New Orleans it was 'jass' music - later corrupted to 'jazz'. Both established themselves first in the bars and, more especially, the brothels. Brilliant young pianists like Scott Joplin and Jelly Roll Morton would play background and sometimes dance music for the girls and their customers. Ragtime music, so called because of the 'ragged' or syncopated style of

playing, was loosely based on the melodic structure of the theatre songs of the period. It soon passed into history, although its heavy left-hand style continued into what later became known as 'stride' piano.

These early musicians brought with them a musical culture quite different from anything else at the time: an unlikely fusion of African tribal chanting and European church music.

From the former came complex and insistent rhythmic patterns, and from the latter the simple harmonies of familiar hymn tunes - specifically the tonic, subdominant, and dominant chords of the major scale (in the key of C, for instance, those chords are C, F and G).

Initially, the only instruments they had to play those chords were on banjos which, in a more primitive form, they had brought with them from Africa, and guitars, which were of European origin.

By the latter half of the 1800s a new secular style had emerged, where instead of singing religious songs musicians sang about the joys and miseries of their everyday lives. The chord sequence was easy enough to be picked or strummed while the important part (the words) could be sung in a way that put the message over. The style used a simple pattern that rounded itself off nicely, with enough variation to keep it interesting.

These vocal laments came to be called 'the blues', and two patterns emerged as the most popular, the 8-bar and the 12-bar blues. In the key of C, and in their most basic form, they look like this:

8-Bar Blues

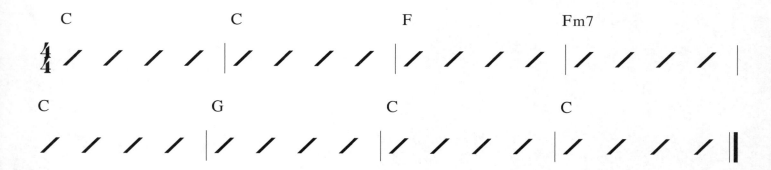

12-Bar Blues

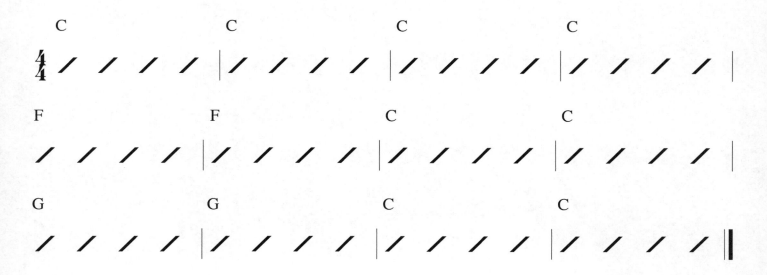

The second one, the 12-bar blues, soon became the most common – you can, after all, say more in 12 bars than you can in eight – and today it is the one most people know.

▶ JIMMY McCRACKLIN

Structures

We've already dealt with the most basic shape, and you'll find that pattern in over half of the original rock 'n' roll songs of the 1950s: *'Rock Around The Clock'*, *'Jailhouse Rock'*, *'Shake, Rattle And Roll'*, etc.

We can now start adding a little colour to our chords. The simplest way is to add a minor seventh to some of them, turning them into dominant sevenths.

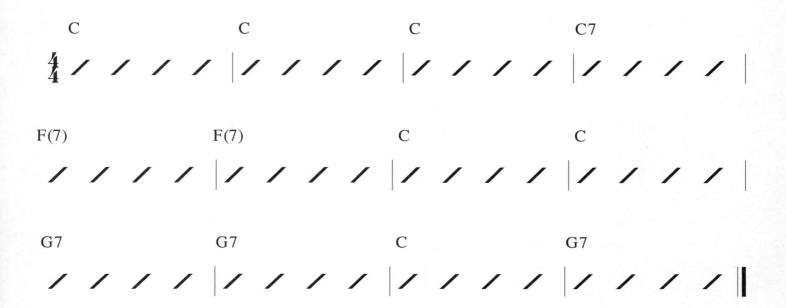

The use of these sevenths helps propel the music towards the next chord change – by adding the seventh you are effectively turning the chord into a temporary dominant seventh, which wants to resolve onto its tonic. For this reason you will find many seventh chords in blues.

In bar 12, there's a G7 now where we had C before: this is to bring us around to the beginning of the next chorus, and it's the simplest way of doing it.

We call this, and any other combination of chords used to get back to the tune, a 'turn-around'.

Think of a blues in C: notice that the third degree of the scale is E natural. When we get to the chord of IV, we add a flattened seventh. This note is E♭, which is the third degree of the minor scale. Early blues musicians picked up on this major/minor flux, and worked it into their melodies.

A simple – and very common – variation is to move to the subdominant (the chord built on the fourth degree of the scale) for bar 2, and then back to the tonic (the chord built on the first degree of the scale).

Again, this is usually done to accommodate a minor 3rd in the tune.

That sequence might look like this:

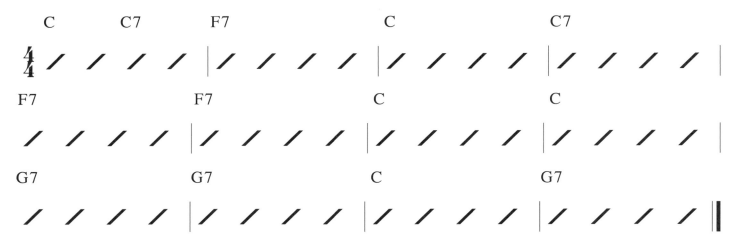

Now, this is all very well as far as it goes; it allows us to look at blues chord progressions in terms of what we can dimly remember from our classroom theory at school.

Unfortunately, those early blues singers didn't have the advantage of a musical education. They sang the way they'd learned from their parents, and that didn't have a lot to do with scales as we know them.

There are a lot of Arab and Indian influences in African music and, as you know, that involves quarter-tones and other strange (to our ears) embellishments. The nearest they could get to that in terms of church harmony was to flatten a few notes in the scale: principally the 3rd, the 5th and the 7th. They frequently sang a minor 3rd against a major chord, and those major chords nearly always contained a minor 7th.

So blues singers – from the very first right up to today – would feel a blues sequence like this:

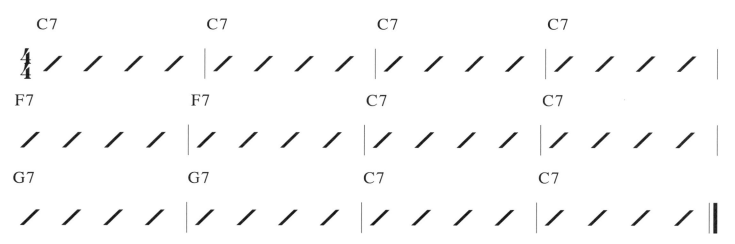

And, almost without exception, this pattern is reflected in left-hand accompaniments to the blues.

As musicians from different backgrounds became involved with blues, they expanded the tunes melodically; and this, in turn, led to the introduction of more chords to accompany this expansion. Some blues sequences started to look like this:

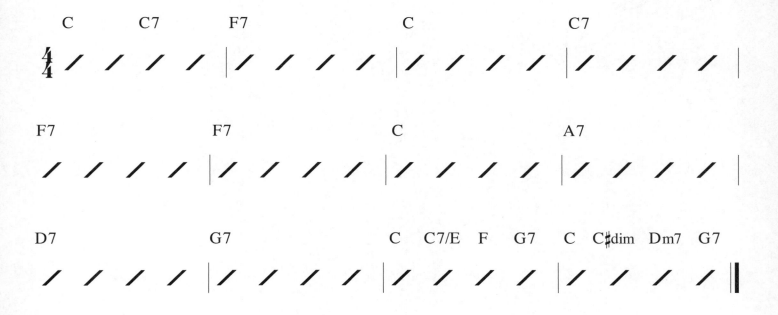

Don't be frightened by the turn-around sequence in the last two bars: you'll normally only get that many chords in a slow blues. C7/E, by the way, is called a 'slash' chord.

It couldn't be simpler: C7 is the chord (left hand or right hand) and E is the bass, or root note.

We talked about the seemingly endless variations of chord structure, and it's certainly true.

Look for instance, at the sequence Ray Charles uses in 'In The Heat Of The Night', a slow gospel-like blues from the title-track of the film:

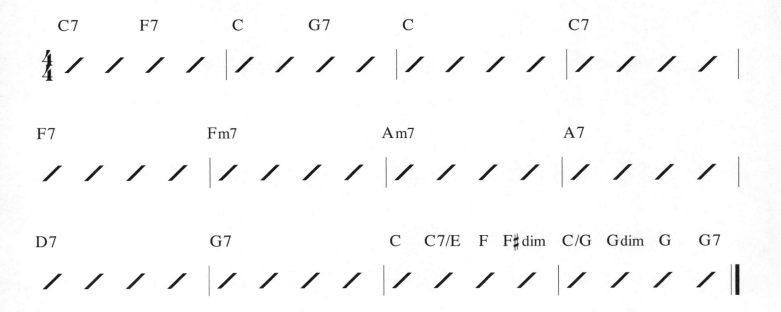

By the end of this book, when you're better acquainted with the 12-bar blues, you'll probably be able to create a few variations of your own.

Basic Blues
Left Hand

For our basic blues, we'll use a slight (but very popular) variation on the first sequence we looked at.

This variation involves substituting an F chord for the second G chord.

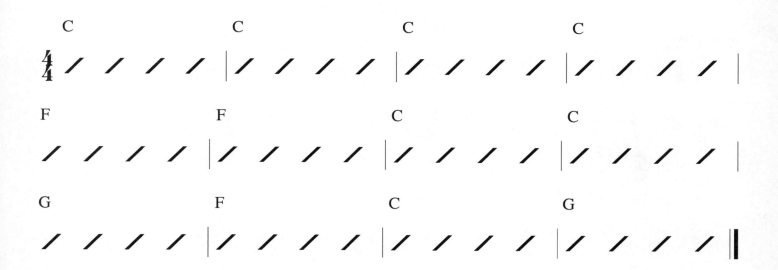

Let's try a simple pattern to begin with.

PRACTISE ALL 3 BASS LINES

TRACKS 1+2

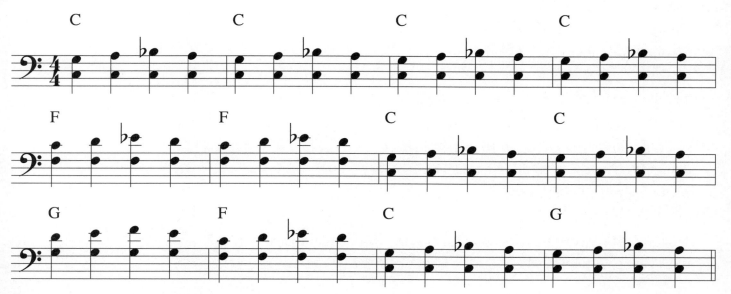

Okay, so this is a very simple pattern: not all that interesting on its own.

But it's easy to memorise, and ideal when you come to adding your right-hand figures because you don't have to think about it too much.

However, this pattern can be thickened up by adding lower thirds to that rising and falling sequence of notes.

Notice how we broke away from the pattern for our 'turn-around', just to emphasise it.

This pattern is also easy to memorise – as, indeed, all successful left-hand patterns must be: you can't concentrate on what your right hand is doing if you're having to think hard about what's happening next in the accompaniment.

So practise these two patterns until you're able to play them automatically.

Basic Blues
Right Hand

What you play with your right hand is, in a way, more important than what happens further down the keyboard.

Whilst the left hand tells your listeners what style you're playing in, and gives a harmonic background to everything your right hand is doing, it's the tune they're listening to, and the things you're able to do with it.

Try playing an easy figure:

Definitely missing something, isn't it?

That missing item is an essential ingredient in the rhythmic make-up of much so-called 'primitive' music from all around the world, especially in music from Africa (and, equally, in the music of Central and South America).

This item is syncopation – the stressing of

normally unstressed accents in a rhythmic pattern: anticipating a beat or coming in behind it, giving the effect of two or more rhythms going on simultaneously.

Now try playing our figure this way – adding a little lick on the end to point out that there's a chord change coming:

Much better, wouldn't you agree?

Now let's repeat it in the minor key, as we
would play it over the IV7 chord:

Just a couple of slight changes are enough
to round off the tune and start it all over again:

MINI
TURN-AROUND

Basic Blues
Both Hands Together

Below, you'll find our tune written out for
both hands – but this time with yet another left
hand pattern.

Practise that first, and then add the right hand,
four bars at a time.

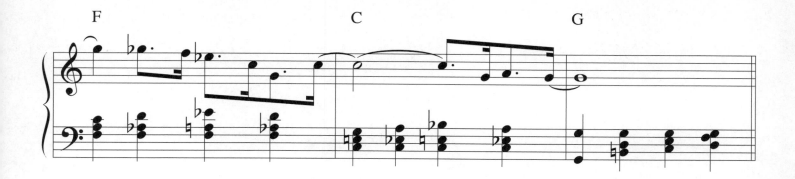

Now try playing this tune with each of the previous accompaniments in turn. Left hand or right hand, you'll have to play one of them from memory.

This is important: reading dots in a blues club or jazz cellar is generally frowned on (or, worse still, laughed at). You can't improvise from written music, only from chord symbols. And, since a 12-bar blues is such a restricted form

(at least as far as its overall shape is concerned), you won't even need a chord chart to work from.

Commit your left-hand patterns and right-hand licks to memory, and just call them up as you need them.

I've added a few other left-hand patterns for you to try out:

You'll see that I've only written out the first bar in each case. By now, you should be able to work out the rest of the sequence from the way our previous patterns were constructed.

Once you've worked them out, try playing the tune with them. When you're comfortable with

this, try adding a few bits of your own to the right hand, or even a different blues altogether.

Finally, for those of you who can stretch that far, we've put in a left-hand pattern in tenths. Don't worry if you can't reach a tenth yet: most people can eventually, with practice.

BIG JOE DUSKIN

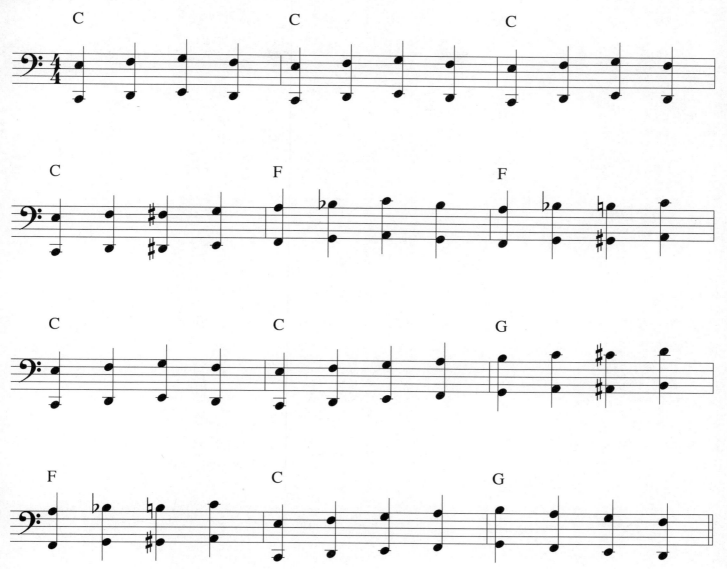

Boogie Piano
Left Hand

We all know what we mean by 'Boogie', don't we? Or do we?

The best we can do to differentiate 'Boogie' from 'Blues' is to say that, in boogie piano, the left hand is a little busier, fussier even, and tends to require 'rolling' the wrist.

Also, its metre is generally eight half-beats to the bar instead of four beats. And there are two ways of 'feeling' it.

One is as a 'straight' eight:

The other way is to 'swing', 'bounce' or 'roll' it; which is by far the commoner of the two.

We've seen this pattern already, as one of our basic blues exercises:

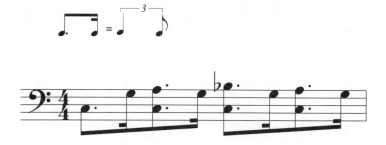

But a more typical early 'boogie' pattern is
produced by 'bouncing' Exercise 1+2 (page 11).

So let's practise this one:

You'll notice that there's no 'turn-around' here.

Left-hand patterns in this particular style are
very hard to play: you have to 'lock in' to them,
grit your teeth and keep going until your arm
drops off.

There's no room for subtleties like turn-arounds!

Boogie Piano
Right Hand

The most important thing to learn about playing 'boogie' piano is that the left hand and the right hand are distinctly separate.

Always work on the left hand first: do it slowly, section by section, until you're totally confident with what you're playing and you can do it almost without thinking.

Only then should you move on to the right hand; so that, if the right hand breaks down because you haven't got it together yet, the left hand will continue on its own.

Try this pattern:

TRACKS 31+32

While you're playing it (slowly at first), beat out the tempo with your right foot. This will enable you to 'swing' with and across the beat, and to lodge the figure in that part of your brain which controls the right hand.

Boogie Piano
Both Hands Together

Now that your left hand and your right hand are fluent separately, the next step is to put them together.

As we have already seen, a 12-bar blues breaks up naturally into three sections of four bars each.

So practise putting your two hands together in four-bar sections.

Let's see how the piece looks in its complete form.

TRACKS 33+34

Now take the right hand part of Exercise 13+14 (page 16) and practise that over your left-hand 'boogie' pattern.

Then try alternating the two different right-hand patterns, and, while you're at it, add a few bits of your own, or, again, a totally different blues tune.

Boogie Piano
Walking Bass

There's another 'boogie' left-hand style that will be very familiar to you: it's known as the 'walking' bass.

In straight eights, it looks like this:

Practise that first; it'll help you to get the finger spacing right, and also get you used to really 'rolling' your wrist.

Now try 'bouncing' it. It's not as difficult as
it looks:

The next step is to play and memorise the
right-hand Exercise 13+14 above it, followed by
Exercise 37+38.

A popular variation (though slightly more
difficult) is demonstrated in the next exercise.
I've added a new right-hand pattern which you
can also use with previous left-hand patterns:

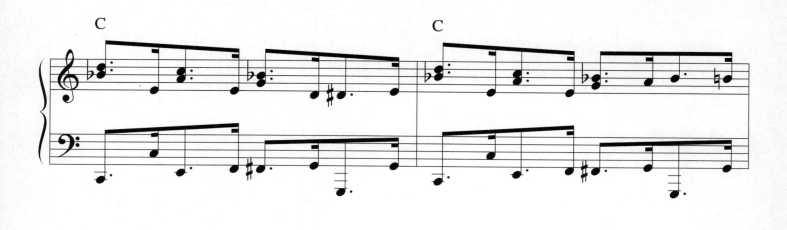

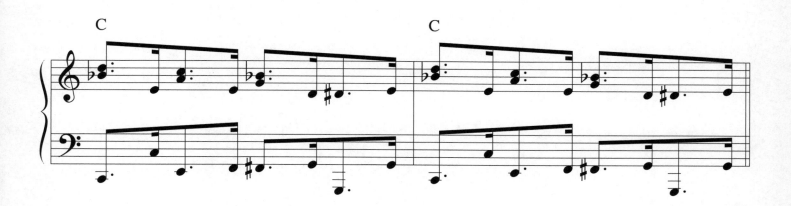

This is what most people think 'boogie-woogie'
is really about.

Stride Piano
Left Hand

In the introduction I referred to 'stride' piano as being a development from 'ragtime'. In fact, as far as the left hand is concerned, there's very little difference between the two.

Continuing with the same 12-bar chord sequence that began our exploration of basic blues, let's try a straightforward exercise:

TRACKS 41+42

Even in this example we can see that the style of playing is rather heavy – lots of octaves and fat chords – which means that there's plenty of scope for bum notes!

Don't rush at it: start slowly and gradually work up your speed.

If you've already played ragtime, or 'classical' marches (waltzes, even), then 'stride' piano should not present too many difficulties for you.

But if you're coming to it fresh, there really is no alternative but to do what we did in the previous exercises – get stuck in, section by

section, and don't try your right hand till the left is completely fluent.

Here's another left-hand pattern, this time with a bit more variation:

TRACKS 43+44

Try a few variations yourself.

Working out chords of your own should not be a problem, but remember to avoid having the root notes remain static – keep them moving up and down.

Stride Piano
Right Hand

We've said that stride piano developed from ragtime, but that the left hand didn't change very much. It was the right hand that changed.

In ragtime, everything was played exactly as written (when it was written down, that is). This was essential in order to produce the rather stately, stylised syncopation required for the type of dance it generally accompanied: the 'ragtime' two-step, played at 'march' tempo.

But, from quite early on, there were a few show-offs who wanted to play the music a great deal faster (much to the consternation of the

great ragtime writers like Scott Joplin and Tom Turpin). At this speed, the right-hand rhythm tended to break away from its previous tight measure – it started to 'swing'.

Instead of dividing into four, the beat now divided into three: ♩ ♪ became ♩ ♪ although it continued (and still does) to be written the same way.

Try this exercise, slowly at first then up to the current speed of your left hand:

When you've got that working steadily, try
playing it over Exercise 41+42 (page 35).

Next we'll try a boogie-type figure in the
right hand:

 TRACKS 47+48

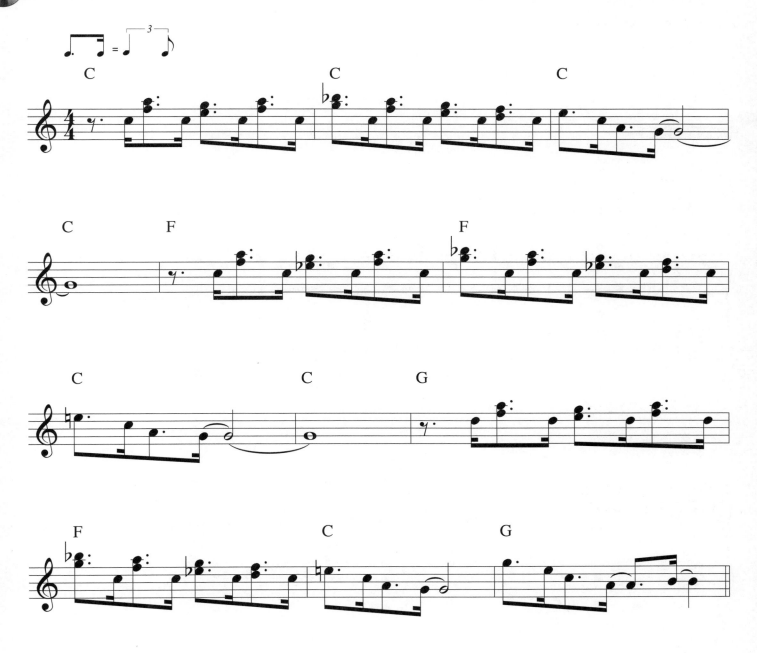

Now try this one over Exercise 43+44 (page 36).

Remember to work at it slowly; but, once
you're feeling confident, try it at speed.

Stride Piano
Both Hands Together

To build something substantial, take Exercise 43+44 (varying it a little if you like) and over it play all the right-hand exercises you've learned so far.

You could finish up with Exercise 47+48, tagging this ending on to it:

TRACKS 49+50

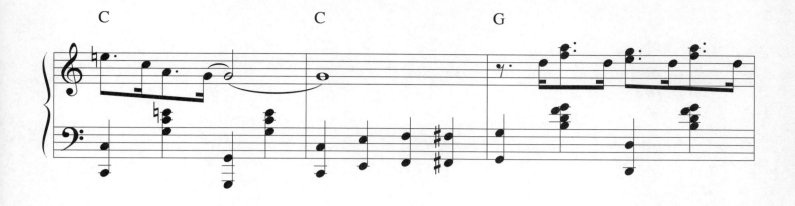

By now you'll have realised that to play really authentic 12-bar blues you have to work quite hard.

Let's move on to something much kinder to your left hand: so-called 'modern' jazz.

Jazz Piano
Some Essential Background

Throughout the 1920s, jazz was the popular music of the day. Dance crazes like the *'Charleston'* and the *'Black Bottom'* flourished everywhere with the help of gramophone records and the new 'wireless'. But changes were going on all the time and, by the 1930s, 'dixieland' jazz had given way to 'swing'.

'Swing' – with the occasional but important exceptions of smaller units fronted by people like Lionel Hampton and Benny Goodman – was essentially big band music.

Unfortunately, by blending with yet more influences (show ballads, 'torch' and novelty songs), this music became too bland for some jazz players – notably Charlie Parker, Dizzy Gillespie and Thelonious Monk – who wanted something a little more challenging to get their teeth into; so, in the early 1940s, they created 'bebop', or plain 'bop', as it came to be known.

But they were still using the 12-bar blues format: *'Blue Monk'* and *'Straight No Chaser'* are just two examples.

The big difference now, however, was the new buzz-word – 'experimentation'.

Instrumentalists, who previously would stick close to the chord-sequence on even their wildest solos, began to base their improvisation on 'modes' rather than keys. There's no room here, alas, to discuss the theoretical basis of this, but one inevitable result was that the poor old piano player was left to provide a harmonic bridge between the increasingly 'avant-garde' soloist and his (sometimes rather puzzled) listeners.

The solution was for the pianist to (a) stop playing root-notes in his left-hand chords (what was the bass player for, after all?) and (b) in changing the shape of those chords ('inverting' them), adding ever more exotic ingredients to colour them: 6ths, major 7ths, flat 9ths, 11ths and 13ths.

Now, a pianist has only so many fingers on his left hand. He can't play all the notes, and so he has to leave a few out. The end result is that some left-hand jazz chords appear, at first sight, to bear little or no relationship to the chord they claim to represent.

But it's not really as complicated as it may seem to you right now. Let's take a closer look.

►► LITTLE BROTHER MONTGOMERY

Jazz Piano
Left Hand

Take a look at this chord:

Bearing in mind that some notes will probably be missing, and that the chord itself may be inverted into any position (i.e. the bottom note doesn't have to be the root note), this chord could be any one of the following:

1. C9, 1st inversion, with the root and 5th missing.

2. Em7(♭5), root position, with the 3rd missing.

3. Gm6, 3rd inversion, with the root missing.

4. B♭(♭5), 2nd inversion, with nothing missing.

Two things will normally dictate what the chord actually is: whatever note the bass is playing, and whichever direction the tune is taking.

The great benefit of this is that you can, more often than not, find your next chord shape adjacent − up or down − to the one you're playing, no matter what that chord is.

Let's have a look at an entirely new 12-bar chord sequence:

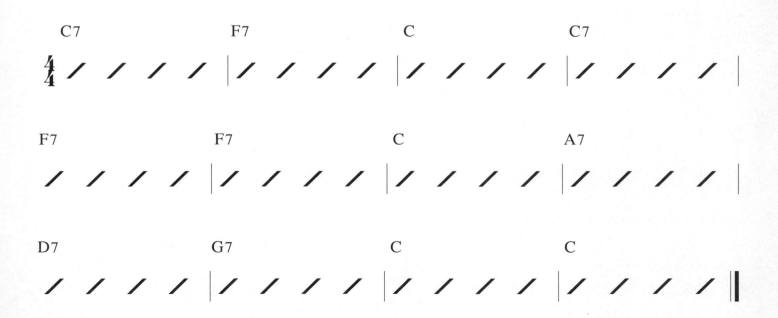

To dress it up, and make it sound more jazzy, we can fatten those chords and make the whole thing much richer.

And, while we're at it, we can add a turn-around, which jazz choruses usually require.

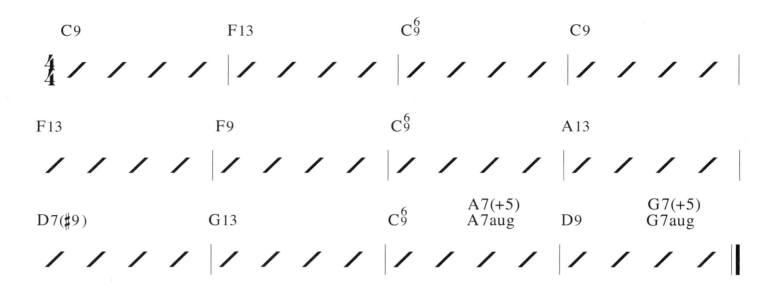

For this sequence our left hand will probably look something like this:

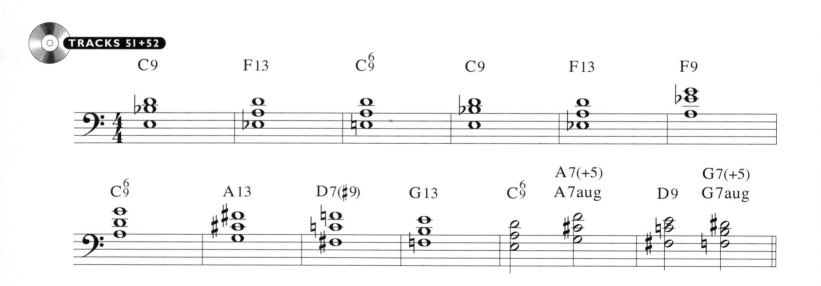

C_9^6 is simply a C chord with an added 6th and 9th (A and D); all the other chords are forms of dominant seventh – we've just added some extra notes for colour.

You may have heard the word 'substitution' when other musicians discuss jazz chords.

The idea itself is very simple.

The two notes which tell you that a chord is a dominant seventh (the two essential ingredients, if you like) are the major 3rd and the minor 7th.

In C7, these are E and B♭.

With this new knowledge, let's take another
look at our turn-around on the previous page.

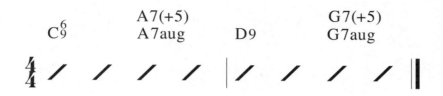

The second chord consists of G, C♯ and F;
if we call the C♯ by its other name (D♭), we
could also have a chord of E♭9. By reversing the
process, the third chord could also be A♭7+.

And, in the same way we looked at the second
chord, that fourth chord also doubles as D♭9.

C : A : D : G	C : E♭ : D : G
C : A : A♭ : G	C : E♭ : A♭ : G
C : A : D : D♭	C : E♭ : D : D♭
C : A : A♭ : D♭	C : E♭ : A♭ : D♭

By a process of permutation, the bass player
could choose any one of a whole series of
four-note patterns, all of which would lead him
back to C:

It's a fascinating area and, given time, it
should be possible for you to work out tritone
substitutions in all 12 keys, for all shapes
of chord.

Jazz Piano
Right Hand

Because of the flexibility and freedom of the left hand in jazz, it becomes possible for the right hand to explore totally new techniques and territory, to create completely different harmonic structures.

But there's no freedom without pain.

If you never did work hard at those scales and arpeggios, you're certainly going to have to now –

for your right hand at least. Just take a deep breath, and think of Oscar Peterson!

For the moment, though, we'll stay with something a lot simpler.

Try this little 12-bar tune:

 **TRACKS 53+54**

Break it down into the usual sections, until the whole thing flows freely.

Jazz Piano
Both Hands Together

Having ploughed through the book thus far, you should be able to put both parts together without looking at the music for your left hand.

But, just in case you really do have the temperament of a true jazzer, and can't be bothered, here are both hands:

TRACKS 55+56

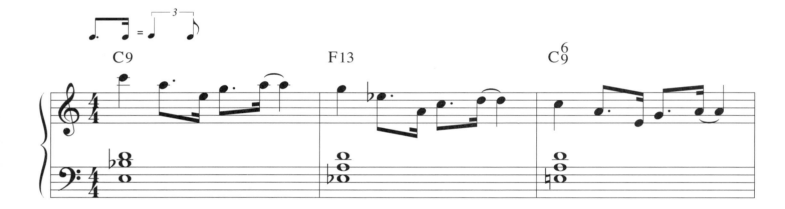

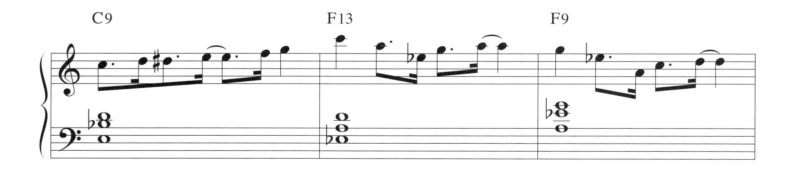

The left hand is a bit static though, as I'm sure you'll agree.

However, with your growing repertoire of chords to call on, you can now play a couple of chords in each bar – most of them different variations of the same chord.

Let's try the tune again with a slightly busier-looking sequence.

Left hand first:

Now with the tune:

Eventually, you'll be able to change chord-shape on every beat, but don't try to do it overnight. Like every other style we've dealt with, do it slowly.

Speed comes with confidence, and confidence comes as your ability gradually (but surely) improves.

► ROOSEVELT SYKES

Rock Piano
Left Hand

'Rock' music appears – and is – less 'sophisticated' than jazz. Most chords tend to be very basic in form, frequently with 'root' notes in straight or broken octaves.

Take, for instance, a tune like '*I Wish I Knew How It Would Feel To Be Free*' – or, as you know it better, the theme tune of Barry Norman's film review programme on television.

The tune itself is pure 'gospel', the chords are a mixture of 'blues' and 'jazz', and the 'feel' is unmistakably 'rock'.

There's nothing wrong with that, of course, except to the most ardent purist. A cross-fusion of two styles, say, almost always works to the advantage of both. It adds 'colour', tension and excitement.

The apparent simplicity of much rock music, though, could lead you into the trap of supposing that it is technically less demanding, and therefore a bit of a 'doddle'. Nothing could be further from the truth.

Whilst the left hand will often stay closer to the bass 'roots' than the bass guitar itself (which will frequently be employed in busy 'passing notes' or even 'counter melodies' in the lower and middle registers), the right hand can be called on to perform tasks every bit as difficult as any to be found in our previous categories.

Let's look at a typical 12-bar rock sequence, which might look like this:

And here's how its left-hand interpretation
could very well be played (remember that we're
no longer 'swinging' the note values: play them
exactly as they read):

▶▶ *GEORGIE FAME*

Rock Piano
Right Hand

You'll have noticed from the chord make-up of our 12-bar rock sequence that the chords themselves are much more straightforward than in any preceding sequence.

The texture of rock music is created by what you add in the way of runs, passing notes, riffs, figures, note-bending and effects generally – including distortion and feedback – to those basic chords.

Whilst the first four are well within the scope of the average pianist, note-bending and effects are not a normal piano remit. But nothing cuts through a rock ensemble more clearly or powerfully than a deep bass octave punched out on an honest 'steam' piano.

Now let's try out a right-hand sequence to go with our left:

TRACKS 63+64

Once you've managed this, try putting both hands together.

Because of the power and volume available to electronic instruments, the principal role of a piano player in rock music is an accompanying one. Deep bass notes and high 'tinkling' phrases will always cut through, no matter now much surrounding 'noise' there is.

And remember, piano is the one thing always called on to carry a rock ballad.

I hope this book has given you some idea of the wide range encompassed by the term '12-bar blues', and of the wonderful versatility possible in tackling that range on a piano.

It's a whole world and, inevitably, we have only scratched the surface but you should by now have a good grounding in what makes a 12-bar blues and, I hope, a new curiosity about ways of exploring the form.

So much of any successful interpretation, however, rests on 'feel' for the style in which you're playing.

There may be some disappointment early on, while you're struggling to get the 'feel' right. But keep persevering.

It really is worth it in the end.

Bluesville

TRACKS 65+66

Mike Morendo

1/12 (181293)